BEING MERCY:
The Path to Being Fully Alive

D1484024

BEING MERCY:
The Path to Being Fully Alive

by

Joseph V. Corpora, C.S.C.

Being Mercy

Copyright © 2019 by Joseph V. Corpora, C.S.C.

10 9 8 7 6 5 4 3 2 1

ISBN 978-1-7321150-4-0

Published by
CORBY BOOKS
A Division of Corby Publishing, LP
P.O. Box 93
Notre Dame, IN 46556

Manufactured in the United States of America

*Dedicated with gratitude to all whom have
shown me the merciful face of God*

Other books by
Father Joe Corpora, C.S.C.

————

The Relentless Mercy of God

Table of Contents

Foreword

In a world that has grown accustomed to division and conflict, in a time when many people doubt whether they are loveable or loved by anyone and in an age that wants us to ignore our sisters and brothers who live on the periphery, Father Corpora reminds us of a better way to live. It is better because it comes from the Lord Jesus Himself. It is the way of divine mercy that brings unity out of division, consolation in our doubts and courage to walk into the shadows of society and stand in solidarity with those in need.

Through his powerful insights, Father Corpora reminds us of the relentless, forgiving and uplifting power of divine mercy that is poured out upon saints and sinners alike. The gift of divine mercy is not offered as something to be received but the life of Someone to be shared, who came into the world as its Savior, freeing us from our sins, fears, doubts and sufferings. For the face of mercy is Jesus Christ and whoever encounters Him will be enlightened in mind, transformed in heart and become an instrument of His mercy, healing and hope in the world.

As you read this book, I invite you to open your heart and to be touched by the divine gift of mercy. May Father Corpora's insights inspire you to trust Christ's healing love in your own life and to become an ambassador of divine mercy in our broken world. In this way we discover the true meaning of the Lord's words: "Blessed are the merciful, for they will be shown mercy" (Mt. 5:7).

Bishop Frank J. Caggiano
BISHOP OF BRIDGEPORT

Introduction

When Pope Francis wrote his Apostolic Letter, *Misericordiae Vultus*, and released it on April 15, 2015, Divine Mercy Sunday, announcing the Year of Mercy, no one could have predicted the revolution of love and tenderness that it would set off in the Church and in the world. Since the first days of his Pontificate, the Holy Father has repeatedly preached and talked about the Mercy of God. He has repeatedly said, "We might get tired of asking God for forgiveness, but God never tires of forgiving us." Pope Francis' will be forever remembered as "the Mercy Pope" and his Pontificate as "a time of mercy for all."

I was very sad to see the Year of Mercy come to a close on the Solemnity of Christ the King, November 16, 2016. It was a truly wonderful Jubilee Year. Along with many others we were hoping that the Holy Father might consider extending the Jubilee Year of Mercy for another year or more.

I was at St. Peter's Basilica in Rome on that day for the closing Mass. I was privileged to concelebrate the Mass. At the end of the Mass, the Holy Father announced that even though the Extraordinary Jubilee Year of Mercy had come to a close that he would ask the Missionaries of Mercy to continue serving the Church as Missionaries of Mercy.

Soon after I received an e-mail from the Pontifical Council for the Promotion of the New Evangelization asking if I wished to continue serving the Church as a Missionary of Mercy. This Pontifical Council "oversaw" the Year of Mercy. I responded immediately that I would be honored and humbled to do so. Then I received a confirmation indicating that Pope Francis commissioned me to serve the Church as a Missionary of Mercy indefinitely.

Even though the Year of Mercy ended two years ago, it has left its mark on the Church and on the world. Pope Francis has truly initiated a revolution of mercy and love that is on going. Why has this revolution of mercy and love continued? We all need mercy.

We all stand in desperate need of God's mercy. No one can live without mercy. You cannot have a world without mercy. In the end I believe that we will all be saved by the free and relentless mercy of God.

Some people will say that all this mercy talk does not allow for justice. This is not true. I have addressed this in a reflection in this book. In his book, *Is This All There Is?*, Gerhard Lohfink writes that "God is completely and all together mercy and just as completely and all together justice—which means that God's justice is mercy and God's mercy is justice."***

God has given me the grace to write about mercy. I never imagined that I would write a book, much less that anyone would buy it. I certainly never thought that I would write a second book. But since there is always more that can be said about mercy, one can keep writing.

Jim Langford suggested the title of this book, *BEING MERCY: The Path to Being Fully Alive*. I immediately liked it. To be fully alive is to be completely given over to God and to the Kingdom. I don't know how one can one give himself/herself completely to God without constantly accepting the relentless mercy of God. Accepting this mercy and being a channel of this mercy is the path to being fully alive.

Every priest has inside of him one core homily. Mine is mercy, the free, relentless, mercy of God. This was true before the Year of Mercy, even more true during the Year of Mercy, and will be true until I preach my last homily, please God.

If you listen to my homilies, this theme will come through again and again. What follows in this little book are more essays and reflections about God's mercy and what it has been like to serve the Church as a Missionary of Mercy. There is no specific order to them. I only hope that the reader will come to know more and more each day that "the mercy of God endures forever..." and then to extend that mercy to others, both near and far.

May Jesus, the face of the Father's mercy, open your life to his relentless mercy as we pray, Lord, Jesus Christ, Son of the Living God, have mercy on me, a sinner.

***Is This All There Is? Gerhard Lohfink, page 155.

Acknowledgments

In February of 2016, at the invitation of John Nagy of Notre Dame Magazine, I begin to write about mercy. He asked if I might write a reflection about mercy every 3-4 weeks for the web version of Notre Dame Magazine. When the Extraordinary Jubilee Year of Mercy ended in November of 2016, John encouraged me to continue writing. And so I did. Much to my own surprise Corby Books published my first book, *The Relentless Mercy of God* in the spring of 2017.

At the end of 2017 Sarah Cahalan took over the role of editing my essays for Notre Dame Magazine. I am indebted to her, as I am to John, for her generous help with editing them. I'm also very grateful to Jim Langford and Tim Carroll of Corby Books for offering to publish them into a second volume.

There are many other people to thank and acknowledge—my parents, Dominick Vito and Evelyn Rose Mosellie Corpora, my brother Jim and my sister Mary Grace. I also wish to thank all those who have read these articles over the past years. Thanks for your encouragement and support.

Most of all I thank God who makes everything possible. Since we all live in God and have our being in God, by thanking God no one is left out.

To God be all glory, honor, praise and thanksgiving now and for ages unending.

Being Mercy:
Being Fully Alive

About 45 years ago—somewhere between the end of the Baltimore Catechism and the new Catechism of the Catholic Church—when Argus posters had won the day as the best source for theology, I heard of St. Irenaeus. One particular poster featured a flower in bloom accompanied by the words, *"The glory of God is man fully alive."*—St. Irenaeus.

I had never heard of St. Irenaeus before, but I really liked the phrase. I remember thinking that I wanted to become fully alive. In my youth at that time, however, I had no idea how hard it would be to become fully alive—in other words, for Christ to be my whole life, my everything. I did not know that it would involve so many deaths and resurrections, so much failure and forgiveness, so much sin and mercy.

Many years have passed since I read those words. There has been a tremendous amount of dying and rising, of sinning and forgiving, more than I ever could have imagined. I have learned many lessons along the way, and I've started to develop a theory on what it means to be fully alive.

I do not think you can become fully alive if you live in a black and white world. To be fully alive, you must be able to live in the gray. In a black and white world, success requires perfection, and the smallest missteps can spell certain disaster. A gray world comes with a safety net: mercy and forgiveness. This safety net makes it possible to fall and fail, but to get up again and again. This safety net makes it possible to trust in God's relentless mercy. You understand that you will fail, and you know that God will catch you. The safety net teaches us that mercy and grace are unmerited, free and abundant. Therese of Lisieux wrote that "everything is grace." The safety net helps us to understand this and that God can work through everything—good and bad—to bring about good.

Being fully alive, I think, also requires a theology of abundance and generosity. There seem to be two theologies of life, one of abundance and generosity, the other of fear and scarcity. A theology of fear and scarcity means that we think that we're going to run out of mercy or love or life or air. The apostles often operated out of fear and scarcity. *How will we ever feed all these people with so little?* And yet we know that their fear was unfounded. In the story of the Loaves and Fishes, not only did they feed the 5,000 members of the gathered crowd, they had more left over afterwards than they had when they started!

The whole world is oriented towards a theology of abundance and generosity. It takes one seed to start a tree and yet millions of seeds fall. This theology of abundance and generosity invites us to give ourselves entirely over to life, to live, to give ourselves, to spend ourselves, to burn out instead of rusting out! A much better idea! A theology of abundance and generosity allows us to fall and to get up, to trust in God's work in our lives and not in our accomplishments.

A wonderful paragraph in the book *The Shoes of the Fisherman* by Morris West reads,

> "It costs so much to be a full human being that there are very few who have the enlight-

or the courage to pay the price. . . .One has to abandon altogether the search for security, and reach out to the risk of living with both arms. One has to embrace the world like a lover, and yet demand no easy return of love. One has to accept pain as a condition of existence. One has to count doubt and darkness as the cost of knowing. One needs a will stubborn in conflict, but apt always to the total acceptance of every consequence of living and dying."

This quotation speaks of a theology of abundance and generosity, a theology of a safety net of mercy and forgiveness. My heart breaks for people who do not have this safety net. Without this safety net, they have to live in a black and white world, no room for failure and growth, no room for dying and rising, and little room for mercy and forgiveness, making it virtually impossible to become a full human being.

If becoming fully alive means Christ being my life, my all, my everything, then we all want it desperately. But we can only get there with a safety net of mercy and forgiveness, with a theology of abundance and generosity. In that abundance and generosity, we are open to the relentless mercy of God, which saves us at every moment of our existence. Being fully alive gives wonderful glory to God, or, as St. Irenaeus put it, is the glory of God. May we all aspire to such a glorious way of living.

Lord Jesus Christ, Son of the Living God,
have mercy on me, a sinner.

Being Mercy:
All the Ends of the Earth

F or several days during the second week of the Christmas season, the Responsorial Psalm comes from Psalm 98, bearing the refrain, "All the ends of the earth have seen the saving power of God."

I recently presided at Mass in the crypt of the Basilica of the Sacred Heart, and as we prayed that refrain, it occurred to me that perhaps the psalmist did not intend "the ends of the earth" to be something physical or geographical. The end of the earth is not Shipshewana. The end of the earth is not at Tierra del Fuego.

The saving power of God—or, to say it another way, the mercy of God—has been extended to each and every person in the world: to those whom we love and to those whom we do not love. The mercy of God has been extended to that coworker whom we wish would get a new job in a faraway country where there are only one-way flights. It has been extended to that priest we wish would become a missionary in Indonesia. And yes, it's even been extended to our mother-in-law. The saving power of God is alive and moving in every person who has ever lived, is living, or will ever live, because God cannot be absent from any person. There is no person outside the saving power of God, no one outside the mercy of God.

In his book *Dare We Hope That All Men Be Saved?*, the Swiss Roman Catholic priest and theologian Hans urs Von Balthasar writes, "If someone asks us, 'Will all men be saved?', we answer in line with the Gospel: I do not know. I have no certainty whatsoever. This means as well that I have no certainty whatsoever that all men will not be saved. The whole of Scripture is full of a proclamation of a salvation that binds all men by a Redeemer who gathers together and reconciles the whole universe. That is quite sufficient to enable us to hope for the salvation of all men without thereby coming into contradiction with the Word of God."

The saving power of God—or, to say it another

way, the mercy of God—has been extended to each and every situation. Nothing is outside of the saving power of God because God cannot be absent from any situation. While it is easy to see God's presence in some situations and not so easy in other situations, God is always present, because God cannot be absent. I do not know how to explain or to understand that God was present when Herod commanded that all the boys in Bethlehem under two years of age should be killed; that God was present at the Holocaust; that God was present in the hurricanes that ravaged countries last year, in the fires of California that caused so much damage, in the battlefields of war; that God was present at Mount Calvary. But the fact that I do not know how to explain God's presence does not mean that it is not true. I believe that the light of the resurrection is burning everywhere. There is no situation outside of God's mercy and God's saving power.

The saving power of God—or, to say it another way, the mercy of God—extends to our very last fault and weakness and flaw and sin. There is nothing outside of the mercy of God. The mercy of God reaches everything, even the dirt under your fingernails, and his saving power extends to our brokenness, our weakness, our fears, our faults, our incompleteness, our sins. God's mercy and God's saving power are so strong that we have nothing to fear. There is no fault or weakness or flaw or sin that is outside of the saving power and the mercy of God.

Of course, we try every day to live a life without sin, to amend our lives, to be converted to God. And one day God will make this happen. What God did for Mary—make her without sin—he will do for us. It's just a matter of time. In the meantime, however, we need to believe and accept and understand that the mercy of God goes deep, right down to every ounce and cell of our being.

This is what we are hoping when we pray that all the ends of the earth have seen the saving power of God. Just as God's saving power extends to Shipshewana and Tierra del Fuego, his mercy extends to every last facet of our lives. Nothing can escape the saving power of God or the mercy of God. How could it? That would be tantamount to saying that there are some things outside of God's careful watch or outside of God's control, which cannot be true.

In this, we can be at peace—not because we have no more progress to make or because we have arrived, but because God is always present and always faithful. And his mercy reaches from age to age, from generation to generation, and to all the ends of the earth.

As the last strains of this psalm die out and we begin a new year, we can rest safely in the loving embrace of a God whose mercy is infinite and relentless. May 2018 be a year of mercy within mercy within mercy.

Lord Jesus Christ, Son of the Living God,
have mercy on me, a sinner.

Being Mercy:
Accepting Forgiveness

———

Two core things about my life enable me to understand the Parable of the Unmerciful Servant, the story in Matthew's Gospel (Matthew 18:21-35) about the king who forgives his servant an enormous debt, only to see that same servant hold a fellow servant accountable for a modest one.

The first thing is that I am a priest. Being a priest does not give me superior intelligence, that's for sure. Rather, in my case, it means that I have heard thousands of confessions over the past 33 years. And I am often sad because people really don't think that God has forgiven them their sins. Not the abortion, the addiction to pornography, the pre-marital sex, the stealing; not the adultery, the cheating on a test, the divorce, the gossip that damages someone's reputation.

I could go on and on. And while I certainly do not want to make light of anyone's sins, I would also not want anyone to make them bigger than God's mercy. Often people imagine their sins are so big that God can't or won't forgive them. But the truth is that God forgives everything, all the time. All our sins and failings, all our transgressions and faults, melt before God's mercy.

In this parable we learn first about a king who forgives everything and then about a man who can't forgive anything. The debt the first servant owes his master, the king, is overwhelming. Since it would be impossible for the servant to pay it off, the king does not even consider asking for repayment. What's more, he listens to his servant's impossible promise to pay, believes his sincerity and writes off the debt altogether. The servant's plea for forgiveness is met with extraordinary mercy.

Then comes the dark side of the story. Seeming to have learned nothing from this incredible experience of mercy, the servant goes out and takes full vengeance on another servant who owes him a much smaller sum than the king had forgiven him. His experience of being forgiven, it seems, has not brought about a change of heart.

I think what's going on here is that the first servant could not accept that he was forgiven. He could not accept in his heart the generosity and kindness and goodness of the king. Failing to believe he is forgiven, he is unable to extend forgiveness of his own.

So sad. And yet, as I noted, I have heard this happen over and over in my life as a priest. People don't think they are truly forgiven. Pope Francis recently said, "Whoever has experienced the joy, the peace and the interior freedom that comes from being forgiven, can open himself in turn to the possibility of forgiving." Sadly, if you cannot accept forgiveness, you might not be able to forgive others.

Now, here's the second thing that helps me understand this parable. I lived in Arizona for 12 years. During that time I crossed the border into Mexico dozens of times. While returning to the United States, I often had conversations with other people walking to cross the border, and I learned that Mexicans always hope the Border Patrol guard they'll encounter is an Anglo, because Mexican-American guards, by reputation, are much harder on Mexicans than the Anglos are.

Now, you can be certain that these Mexican-Americans were themselves immigrants at one time. Rough experience, though, suggests these guards have forgotten all about that. So many of us have forgotten the immigration chapter in our family's history.

The unwelcoming person is also an ungrateful person. How could the first servant in Jesus' parable be grateful when he refuses to forgive his fellow servant? If we want instead to be like the king we must accept and be grateful for God's constant mercy. When we do, we will not mistreat our companions, no matter what we think they owe us.

More than anything else, the parable reminds us of our constant need to recall our own experiences of being forgiven and to consider how these encounters have influenced our behavior. God's mercy is limitless. It never ends. The Holy Father always reminds us priests, "When you enter the confessional to hear confessions, first recall your own great need to be forgiven."

True forgiveness means setting aside measured or

calculated thinking. It means not withholding for-giveness, no matter how much we hurt, or how long it takes to fade. It means not weighing the other person's "merit," whether they've "earned" it, before we forgive. It even means not waiting until that person asks our forgiveness before we decide to forgive. We should be the first to act and to offer forgiveness. God always is.

A king ready to forgive all, and a servant willing to forgive nothing. What a twist of events. What an unexpected outcome. If anyone should be willing to overlook another's debt, you'd think it would be the simple man, not the king. But this story is a parable. It is intended to subvert our way of thinking. It turns out God is far more generous and merciful and compassionate and forgiving than any of us could ever hope to be. But we can try. We must.

Lord Jesus Christ, Son of the Living God,
have mercy on me, a sinner.

Being Mercy:
Best!

In his second letter to the Corinthians, Paul writes words that have both consoled and perplexed Christians of all eras. He says: "For when I am weak, then I am strong." These words can sometimes sound nice—maybe even holy, in spiritual conversations—but what could they possibly mean in our day-to-day lives that so revolve around strength, racing to the top and staying there, and being number one?

"For when I am weak, then I am strong."

We live in a world where people sign off on emails and letters with the word "best." What does this mean? Best? Best what? Best Buy? Best show on the road? Best in Show at the 4-H Fair? Best chili in Texas? Best show in town? I often wonder what all those people are doing with the time that they are saving by not writing Best Wishes or Best Regards. In reaction to the deluge of "bests," I often sign off with "Average" or "In the 15th percentile."

You might think that I'm making something out of nothing. Though I would often like to be God, I'm not—so I'll leave the making something out of nothing to Him! I think that the use of the word "Best" is a real problem. It gets into our consciousness in a way I think is ultimately unhealthy, and it can encourage us to not be honest about our weaknesses or faults or failings and the very important role that they can play in our lives. After all, we want to be best. That doesn't leave much room for faults and weaknesses.

Here's another example from our modern life. Every workshop, every conference, every meeting you go to now eventually deals with "best practices." When I submit a proposal to talk at a conference, I often note that I am going to talk about "worst practices." Most of us have learned more from our failures than from our successes. Most of have learned much more from what we have done wrong than from what we have done correctly. And yet there is such an aversion to talking about "worst practices."

The Church has always taught that there are certain kinds of success that grow best in the soil of failure.

If we did not learn from our failures, from our worst practices, from our sins, then what purpose would the Cross have? Why would we hold the Cross as central to our lives? Why would we say, as we do in the Congregation of Holy Cross, that the Cross is our only hope? To say that the Cross is our only hope is not poetry. The Constitutions of the Congregation of Holy Cross say that "there is no failure that the Lord's love cannot reverse." Like our "Ave Crux Spes Unica" motto, this is not a sentimental thought. It's the truth.

To believe that the Cross is our only hope, to believe that there is no failure that the Lord's love cannot reverse is to believe and hope with our whole being that "when I am weak, then I am strong."

Perhaps the sin that people most often confess is that they are judgmental. A close second, and a sibling of the same sin, is pride. "Father, I'm a proud person. Father, I'm prideful." So many of us struggle with this sin.

Fortunately there is a remedy for being judgmental and prideful. But no one likes it. Depending on your degree of pride, God gives you (as he gave St. Paul) a thorn in your side to, as Paul put it, "keep you from being too elated." God is faithful to each one of us, so make no mistake, he will give you a thorn—a sin that you cannot conquer, a fault you cannot fix, a weakness you cannot turn a corner on.

You will try. You will struggle with this thorn your entire life. To get past it, you will go forward and backward, backward and forward, up and down, down and up, even sideways! God will give this to you so that you don't get too taken with your greatness —to keep you from being too elated. Living with this thorn in your side, living with this sin and weakness will make you long for and yearn for and desire the mercy of God.

This fault, this sin, this weakness, whatever it is, will keep you grounded in humility. It will keep you close to the earth, close to others, close to yourself, and even close to God. You can, of course, deny this weakness, pretend that you don't have it. This will increase your pride and your judgmental tendencies, and make you otherwise impossible to live with and be around.

The key is that you have to acknowledge and accept—even embrace—this weakness, fault, failing, or sin. Don't take this the wrong say as though I am saying "sin is good." I am not saying that exactly. What I am saying is that sin can have a purpose in our lives. As we say in Spanish, *"Dios se vale de todo."* God makes use of everything.

Do not despair. Do not quit. Do not give in. In the midst of Paul's struggle with the thorn in his side, while he is begging Jesus to take this thorn from him, Christ tells him, "My grace is sufficient for you, for my power is made perfect in weakness."

This passage from the second letter of St. Paul to the Corinthians is so consoling, so hopeful, so reassuring to those who know themselves as sinners. We are sinners whose sins are forgiven by God, sinners who know that God's mercy can make us strong even in our sinfulness.

God, in his mercy, is always at work in our lives, always accomplishing his word and his work in us. Denying or running away from your weaknesses, faults, failures and sins might make you miss out on all that God can do in your life and with your life. You might never know what it can mean for his power to be made strong in your weakness. Trusting in God's relentless and boundless mercy makes it possible for us to embrace our whole self and to allow God's life and power to shine through our weaknesses—and oh, how much good it can accomplish.

It might even keep you from signing your emails "best."

Lord Jesus Christ, Son of the Living God,
have mercy on me, a sinner.

Being Mercy:
Conversion

Every year, the Church celebrates the Feast of the Conversion of St. Paul, the Apostle, on January 25. When we hear the words "conversion of St. Paul," most often we think of the reading from the Acts of the Apostles, chapter 22, verses 3-16. The passage tells how Saul had been persecuting the followers of Jesus when he was knocked off his horse by a blinding light. As we hear in the Scripture, he eventually becomes a follower of Jesus under the new given name Paul, and he goes on to spend the rest of his life spreading the faith everywhere he can.

But what does conversion mean? From what is Paul converted? I recently read a reflection from Sister Ruth Burrows, OCD (a Carmelite nun at Quidenham, Norfolk, England), that helped me understand

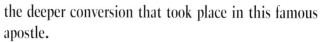

the deeper conversion that took place in this famous apostle.

Let's look more closely at the conversion of St. Paul. To speak of Paul's conversion as the conversion of a sinner in the sense that we usually mean is inaccurate. This is not like the conversion of Alessando Serenelli, who murdered Maria Goretti. While serving 27 years in prison for his crime, Serenelli reported seeing a vision of his victim in which she repeated to him how she had forgiven him on her deathbed. From this point, he was converted and became a model prisoner. Upon his release, he worked as a gardener and porter in a convent of Capuchin friars.

Paul was not a sinner in this sense. Rather, he was a deeply religious man, a devout Jew, and was blameless in the keeping of the law. He strove for purity of heart. Paul was not a hypocrite, not an outward boaster like the Pharisees that are portrayed in the Gospels. He acted from a sincere heart.

The sudden encounter with the Lord that we hear about in the reading from Acts turned his whole world upside down. To Paul, the story of Jesus was a revolting scandal. A man crucified as a criminal and condemned by the law was, in fact, God's Messiah and Promised One? How could this be? Everything about Paul's world was turned upside down by this revelation. Maybe this is why he had to be knocked off his horse—so that he could see correctly!

This is hard for us to understand, because we revere the Cross and see it as our most hopeful sign, the sign of our redemption. We wear the cross around our neck; it hangs in our homes, and is present in every classroom at Notre Dame, and in countless other places.

But, to Paul, it was the exact opposite of every idea he had of the God of his ancestors and of the Messiah that he was waiting for. The encounter with Jesus changed all this in one second. The cross became the center of his existence, the only content of his preaching, the truth that he constantly boasted of and gloried in.

Paul accepted this with all his heart, and God was able to give him the fullness of His offerings. Paul gave up everything before the crucified Jesus, everything that he had been proud of—his Hebrew ancestry, his training, the righteousness he had acquired through self-discipline and effort. All of it was thrown out.

All of it now counted for nothing. Paul saw that all this did not give him an ounce to claim God's love. He saw clearly that no human being could earn God's love or could win God's approval or could merit anything from God.

This is his real conversion. This is what Paul was converted from—from thinking that he could earn or merit or win his salvation to freely accepting all that God wanted to give him.

God gave his love freely in and through the man Jesus. As part of his conversion, Paul was freed of all righteousness of his own. After the encounter in Acts, his only righteousness is that which comes through Jesus, only that which is given by Jesus freely and generously and without cost. Paul could boast of none of his accomplishments. He could only boast of what God had done for him.

So this is the real conversion that Paul underwent —from a life of thinking that he could earn and win and merit God's love by observing every part of the law to accepting all that God offered. Paul had believed that, if he behaved well, always did the right thing, and knew the law inside and out, he could earn

God's love. In the moment of his conversion, he came to see that this was not true at all.

God's love, made manifest to us in Jesus, is freely and generously and gratuitously given. Paul came to understand this truth in his conversion, and so must we undergo this conversion in our own lives. We all need to be converted from thinking that we can earn or merit or gain or barter for our salvation. We all desperately need to simply accept the goodness and generosity of God and let God give us all that He wants to give us. Our only role is to accept what God has to offer—ultimately, what God desperately wants to give us.

Maybe, someday, each of us will have our own feast day—the Conversion of St. Lily, the Conversion of St. Conor, the Conversion of St. Colleen, the Conversion of St. Geoff—that celebrates our real conversion, our move from trying to earn God's love to freely accepting it, and then being grateful for it and wanting to share it. As we enter the season of Lent, may it be for all of us a season of this true conversion, like St. Paul's.

Lord Jesus Christ, Son of the Living God,
have mercy on me, a sinner.

Being Mercy:
Everything Belongs

I think everyone would like to go to their graves having no regrets in their lives. Wouldn't you like to be on your deathbed feeling grateful for everything that has been in your life and not regret anything? This can only happen if you accept the mercy of God, always and forever, freely given.

Consider St. Matthew's parable that we all know as the "Parable of the Wheat and Weeds":

The kingdom of heaven may be likened to a man who sowed good seed in his field. While everyone was asleep his enemy came and sowed weeds all through the wheat, and then went off. When the crop grew and bore fruit, the weeds appeared as well. The slaves of the householder came to him and said, "Master, did you not sow good seed in your field? Where have the weeds come from?" He answered, "An enemy has done this." His slaves said to him, "Do you want us to go and pull them up?" He replied, "No, if you pull up the weeds you might uproot the wheat along with them. Let them grow together until harvest; then at harvest time I will say to the harvesters, 'First collect the weeds and tie them in bundles for burning; but gather the wheat into my barn.'" (Matthew 13:24-30)

Those listening to the parable would have been surprised to hear Jesus' saying, "Let the weeds and the wheat grow together until harvest." And why? Because you might not know one from the other, Jesus clearly implies: "If you pull up the weeds you might uproot the wheat along with them."

Is it too much to say that everything you have ever lived and done and tried, whether you succeeded or failed, has purpose and meaning in your life? Let God determine what is what. That's not really our job. Our job is to accept everything that is part of our life and to trust that God knows why everything that's in our life is in our life.

The definition of a weed is something that does not belong. A blade of wheat in a rose garden is a weed. A rose in a wheat field is a weed. This parable is an invitation from God to trust that everything that is in our life belongs in our life. In the end God will remember all the good we have done and will launder the bad so as to make it clean and good.

We'll all be shocked when we get to heaven and are able to see our life as God sees it—that is to say, with the eyes of God—to find out that the very things we would have uprooted actually belonged in our lives, and not only belonged, but were the very things through which God saved us.

The poet Rainer Maria Rilke wrote, "Be patient toward all that is unsolved in your heart and try to love the questions themselves, like locked rooms and like books that are now written in a very foreign tongue. Do not now seek the answers, which cannot be given you because you would not be able to live them. And the point is, to live everything. Live the questions now. Perhaps you will then gradually, without noticing it, live along some distant day into the answer."

God wants us to get to the point in life where we come to accept everything that has happened in our life as belonging there. A failed marriage? Mental illness? A job I was fired from? Something I was unfairly accused of? A pattern of sin I am unable to turn a corner on? I am not saying these are necessarily good things. I am not putting any label on them. I am only suggesting that they might be in our life for some reason, that God can work through them, that God can bring life through whatever is the truth of our life.

God will determine what is wheat and what is weeds, and he will then separate one from the other. And he will do this in his time and in his way. Were it up to us we might uproot the very experience, the very truth—as painful as it might be—that is in fact saving our lives.

God is present at every moment of our existence, independent of the content of the moment. God is always present. God is in all things. It is not possible to say that God is more present in this than in that. God is always present.

God is equally present when the doctor tells us that our cancer is in remission as when the doctor tells us that our cancer has returned. God is equally present when the parish community gathers for a parish mission as when two or three prisoners on death row call upon him for help. God is equally present when a woman is giving birth as when a woman is having an abortion.

This does not mean that all things are equal or have the same value. But it does mean that God is always present. And no one can say that God is more present in this situation than in that one. You cannot quantify God's presence, for he is always present. Another way of saying the same thing is this: God cannot be absent.

So everything that is in your life belongs there. This is another way of saying that God is saving you through everything that has ended up in your lap— whether you chose it or whether it came to visit you. This does not mean it's all easy or fun. It only means that God has chosen it for you, or for some unknown reason has allowed it to visit your life. And, for the most part, you don't know whether it will turn out to be weeds or wheat. You don't have to know. You only have to believe that God knows and will separate out the wheat from the weeds at harvest time.

We have to accept the lives God has given to us. And for the most part that means learning to live with wheat and weeds, and with not knowing which is which. God will take care of this in his time and his way.

If we can accept this truth, we stand a chance of going to our graves not regretting anything. Instead, we may be thankful for all that has ended up in our lap—because, as St. Therese of Lisieux says over and over, "Everything is a grace." She doesn't decide what is and what is not. Rather, she says, everything is a grace. If we follow her lead, we will meet the Lord with no regrets.

Lord Jesus Christ, Son of the Living God,
have mercy on me, a sinner.

Being Mercy:
Everything Matters

F or several years now I've said that the older I get, the better I look in gray. At first, people chuckle. But I'm very serious about it. I used to worry this meant I was moving to a position where nothing mattered. The truth is quite the opposite: Everything matters, and that's why things look more gray than black or white.

Let me explain. God is involved in every detail of our life, so everything matters. And if everything matters, then things will necessarily be messy. A messy life means a gray life, not a black and white one.

I keep running across things people say and write that speak to this grayness I see. In a passage about the life of St. Augustine in his excellent *New York Times* bestseller, The Road to Character, columnist David

Brooks quotes Reformed theologian Lewis Smedes: "Our inner lives are not partitioned like day and night, with pure light on one side of us and darkness on the other. Mostly, our souls are shadowed places; we live at the border where our dark sides block our light and throw a shadow over our interior places.... We cannot always tell where our light ends and our shadow begins or where our shadow ends and our darkness begins."

A student in Dillon Hall, where I happily live, writes a quote on his dry-erase board every day. Recently he shared this thought, attributed to Nikola Tesla: "Our virtues and our failings are inseparable, like force and matter. When they separate, man is no more." So interesting.

Both quotes suggest that life is more gray than black or white. If we are honest about our lives, we see how they are a mixture of day and night, of light and darkness, of virtues and failings, often inextricably bound together. As with a difficult surgery, it may be almost impossible to take something out without damaging something else. Often surgeons opt not to remove a tumor because the danger of damaging something good is so great that it's better to leave it alone.

In the moral life, we want so badly to eradicate our sins and shortcomings. I often think God must have a reason for allowing me to fail, because he certainly knows that I desire to eradicate sin from my life. He knows I sweat blood trying to do so and yet I still fail. Could it be that in eradicating a certain sin, I might also eradicate a virtue? Or, worse yet, that I would feel proud for having overcome it?

I often tell students in the confessional that, whatever they're struggling with, God will not act until they're convinced they can't do it on their own. At the moment they surrender, he will step in and take care of it. In the meantime, we learn to live in the grayness of life.

In a previous essay, I referred to the parable of the wheat and the weeds in Luke's Gospel. Workers inform their landowner that an enemy has sewn weeds among the wheat. They ask if they should uproot the weeds. The landowner replies, "No. Wait until harvest time, because at this point you might not be able to tell the wheat from the weeds." Might we find the same difficulty with telling our light from our darkness, our virtues from our failings?

So we come to Advent. In reflecting on this season of waiting, spiritual author James Finley says that even though there was no room at the inn, "God came anyway. The fact there was no room in the inn did not stop God from being born into this world."

In our lives filled with clutter and chatter, with unfinished business and rough edges, with cell phones and bitmojis, it often seems we have no room at the inn. We barely keep ahead of the day's demands and messiness, all of which is necessarily gray. God is not waiting for our lives to be pure light, pure white, pure virtue so he can be born into them. Rather, as Finley says, "God is being born unexplainably in our hearts moment by moment, breath by breath." We find him in the "interior richness of every little thing that happens to us and everyone around us."

Why are we so afraid of gray? Why do we strive for black and white when we know things aren't that way? Maybe it's because we want to live with certitude. Yet, when certitude lessens the need for faith, it can be a problem.

As I get older the only thing I am sure of—or at least as certain as a person can be in this life—is the

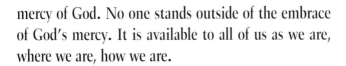

mercy of God. No one stands outside of the embrace of God's mercy. It is available to all of us as we are, where we are, how we are.

Lord Jesus Christ, Son of the Living God,
have mercy on me, a sinner.

Being Mercy:
Good Friday in the Prison

O n Good Friday I had the unique privilege of presiding and preaching at Westville Prison, about an hour west of South Bend. Fifty men live in the dorm where we had the Good Friday prayer service, all of them enrolled as students through an initiative of the University and Holy Cross College. I am so impressed with this initiative. It is really a time-honored way of understanding education and learning—the men get to discuss what they're learning and studying in class in their day-to-day conversations in the dorm, and along the way, they can earn Bachelor's or Associates degrees. This year, on May 24, three men will receive a BA, and 17 men will receive an AA.

My visit began in the common room of the student dorm, where I tried to meet and shake the hand of each person present, some men I had met before in my last visit, others I had not.

As I did this, I could not help but think of what Pope Francis says on his annual Holy Thursday prison visits in Rome: "There is really no good reason why I am not in here and you are not out there." I think of my own life. The major reasons why I am not inside have almost nothing to do with me.

I had good parents who brought me up a certain way and were always there for me. I did not choose my parents.

I grew up in a lower middle class neighborhood that was safe and where everyone looked out for each other. I did not choose that neighborhood.

I went to Catholic school from kindergarten to eighth grade and received a great education at the hands of the Salesian Sisters of St. John Bosco, an education and formation that I will never be able to be sufficiently grateful for. I did not choose to go to that school.

Any differences in those three things, over which I had no control, could have put me on a very different trajectory in life. I could be on the inside.

Before I went to the prison, I thought about what Gospel I would use and what I would preach on. I decided to preach from the Gospel of Luke (23:32-34).

"Now with Jesus they were also leading out two other criminals to be executed. When they reached the place called The Skull, they crucified him there and the two criminals also, one on the right, the other on the left. Jesus said, "Father, forgive them; they do not know what they are doing."

I wanted the Gospel and homily to reach the hearts of the guys in prison, to offer some hope and consolation. After reading the Gospel, I said, "We all know these words spoken by Jesus shortly before he died on the Cross. 'Father, forgive them; they do not know what they are doing.'

"What do these words mean?" I asked. "Of course the Roman soldiers knew what they were doing. They had scourged Jesus. They had put a crown of thorns on his head. They had insulted him and were making fun of him. They were nailing him to a cross. They were putting a human being to death. They knew exactly what they were doing."

The words of Jesus show a divine generosity that is

surprising and so consoling. It is as if the Lord wants to go further than we could ever go to excuse us. He will find any reason to relieve us of the burden of guilt, if he can. And notice that the Roman soldiers do not even ask for forgiveness, yet Jesus asks his Father that it should be given to them.

"What might these words mean for us?" I asked. "Father, forgive them; they do not know what they are doing." We all do wrong. We all sin. We all do things that we shouldn't do. We all fail to do things that we should do. We cause evil in the world. The damage to ourselves and to others that comes from the wrong that we do and the good that we do not do is real.

But for the most part we are innocent. Not because we do not know that what we are doing is wrong —we do know—but because we do not know how much we are loved. We do not know how much we are held in love by God. This is what we do not know.

When Jesus asks his Father to forgive his executioners on the basis of their ignorance—"they do not know what they are doing"—Jesus is asking that they be forgiven because they did not know that they

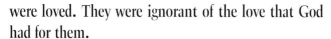

were loved. They were ignorant of the love that God had for them.

Not realizing that we are unconditionally loved is the real darkness, the real ignorance. When we sell ourselves short, when we hurt others or damage their reputation, when we settle for second best, when we abandon our ideals, or fill with rage or jealousy... when we do these things, we usually know that we are doing wrong.

What we don't know is how much we are loved and cherished. We are not so much bad or malicious. Rather we are wounded and despairing of love.

We will finally realize that we are sinning not when we know the law or when we are experts at moral questions, but when we sense how much we are loved and how precious we really are. Until that happens, we continue living in the darkness that lets us go on crucifying Christ, crucifying others, and crucifying ourselves.

Christ died for us on the cross so that we would never be without the experience of someone falling in love with us, and to reveal more fully how much we are held in love by our God. I told the men, "For sure,

God has fallen in love with each one of us. You don't die on the Cross for someone if you don't love them."

Forgiveness is one of God's most beautiful qualities, and it's equally beautiful among ourselves. I said to the men, "Though I do not live here at Westville, I am certain that you have the opportunity to forgive one another on a daily basis and to allow some trust to develop among yourselves." I further explained that I live in a dorm with 300 undergraduates. We have the opportunity to forgive one another and to renew trust among ourselves on a regular basis.

I ended the homily by saying, "I hope that when you look at Christ on the cross, you believe and know even more how deeply you are held in love and cherished by God."

After the homily I invited the men to offer any petitions. Many did. I had to fight back tears when they prayed, "for my children," "for all those on the outside whom I have let down," "for the poor and the suffering," "for my family." After the petitions, we had a closing prayer. I shook hands again with most of the guys and, to a person, they all thanked me for coming. I kept saying, "Thanks for having me."

I am so encouraged by a God who is so merciful that he is always willing to look for ways to relieve us of the burden of guilt that we all carry—a God who loves us so much that he offers his forgiveness and his mercy even when we don't ask for it. Just as he did on the cross, Jesus himself is always asking and granting that mercy for us, because, like the men at Christ's crucifixion, we do not know just how loved we are.

Lord Jesus Christ, Son of the Living God,
have mercy on me, a sinner.

Being Mercy:
It's All Good

S omeone bumps into someone in the supermarket, "Oh, I'm sorry," says the first person. "No worries," the second person says, "It's all good." A student helps another student carry some books and accidentally drops them. "Oh, sorry about that," says the first student. "It's okay," the second one says, "It's all good."

To be honest, I don't like the phrase. But you hear it everywhere and I'm guessing it's going to be around for a while.

Somewhere along the way it got into our minds and hearts that the goal in the life of any serious Christian is to stop sinning or to get beyond sin. I hear it all the time when I meet with sincere and earnest students. I hear it from people who take their life in Christ seriously.

We say it in the Act of Contrition. "I firmly resolve with the help of thy grace to *sin no more* and to avoid the near occasions of sin." If we are honest, even as we say those words, we feel a little inauthentic, because we're fairly certain that we're going to sin again.

Last Sunday I was traveling, so I went to an early Mass at Sacred Heart Parish in the crypt of the Basilica at Notre Dame. And for some reason, the words the priest spoke at the beginning of Mass, words that I myself have said tens of thousands of times when I preside at the Eucharist, really struck me. "Let us call to mind our sins to prepare ourselves to celebrate these sacred mysteries." And then, of course, we ask God's mercy upon us.

> *Lord, have mercy.*
> *Christ, have mercy.*
> *Lord, have mercy.*

Two competing views?

On the one hand we promise to try to sin no more, and on the other we say we cannot begin celebrating these sacred mysteries without first calling to mind our sins. Is it possible that we cannot even think about truly celebrating the Mass without knowing

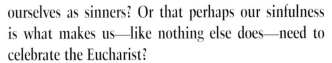

ourselves as sinners? Or that perhaps our sinfulness is what makes us—like nothing else does—need to celebrate the Eucharist?

We all know truths like this: God does not save us as saints. Rather he saves us as sinners. In the Hail Mary, we say, "Pray for us sinners, now and at the hour of our death. Amen." The Lamb of God that we pray at every Mass repeats, "Have mercy on us." Moments before we receive Holy Communion, we pray, "Lord, I am not worthy that you should enter under my roof, but only say the word and my soul shall be healed." And in *Luke 5:32* we read, "I have not come to call the upright but sinners to repentance."

Our daily lives are filled with a constant awareness of our sinfulness and our desperate need for God's mercy, and reminders that God's mercy is infinite.

Maybe when we say, "I firmly resolve with the help of thy grace to *sin no more*" while reciting the Act of Contrition, we should pray instead, "I firmly resolve with the help of thy grace to *accept my sinfulness and trust that in God's mercy even my sins will lead me to him*."

I always say that as long as I am alive the Church

will fulfill her mission to forgive and welcome sinners. Oh, don't get me wrong. I would love to stop sinning. I have not given up on this. Actually I won't stop sinning, but God will bring me to a point where I no longer sin. From all evidence that will not be in this life, rather it will be in the life to come. I can wait and trust. In this life, I will continue to sin and I will continue to trust in God's mercy and in God's forgiveness.

I think it would be better if we began thinking this way. Some might say this would give us license to stop trying, to stop caring. Hardly. What it would do is to help us know much more deeply that we exist and depend entirely on the mercy of God. That's the truth.

Next month will mark one year since the Extraordinary Year of Mercy ended. And yet as the Holy Father has noted, the fruits of that year continue to flourish. I think one of those fruits might be just this: That we would all become that much more aware that God's mercy endures forever and that we will need it forever.

And maybe that overused phrase has it right: It's all good. That doesn't mean sin is good. But it can mean that the way that God uses our sin is good.

It's all good.

Lord Jesus Christ, Son of the Living God,
have mercy on me, a sinner.

Being Mercy:
Judgment or Mercy

The most common sin that I hear in the confessional is one of being judgmental. "Father, I'm 84 years old and I'm critical of my grandchildren's spouses." "Father, I'm always judging my mother-in-law about everything and at every step of the way." "Father, I'm judgmental towards whole groups of people."

I often tell the penitent the Story of the Red Car. It goes like this.

Once upon a time I came out of a store and got into my car. While I was inside, a red car had parked in front of me, so close to my car that I couldn't get out of the spot. I could tell the car was running, but the driver had apparently run into the store. After a few minutes waiting, I got impatient. I noticed that there was a passenger in the car. And I thought to myself: "If that passenger would just hop into the driver's seat and pull the car up a foot or two, I would be able to maneuver my way out." The passenger, however, did not move into the driver's seat. So I started to beep at the passenger, hoping that she would take the hint, get out of the passenger seat, move into the driver's seat and pull the car up. Nothing doing. The longer I waited, the angrier I became.

I decided to get out of my car, go to the passenger and ask her—maybe politely, maybe not—to move the car. I knocked on the car window, ready to be snarky and ask her to get into driver's seat and move the car. She turned to smile at me, and it was then that I noticed that she was blind.

That put me in my place. Here I was, getting angrier by the second, making all sorts of judgments about her not moving to the driver's seat, and she was blind. Had I known that, of course, I would never have beeped at her, gotten out of my car, or thought to yell at her. I might still have been annoyed, but I would have been patient.

When we judge someone, it's always true that if

we knew one more thing about that person or had one more piece of data, we might think very differently. If we knew what happened to this person when he was in fourth grade.... If we knew what happened to that person when her family moved across the country and she had to start all over again in high school. . . .If we knew that his parents had divorced when he was young and was raised by his grandparents.... If we had one more piece of information, we would make very different judgments or not judge at all.

We already think this way about ourselves: "If that person knew this or that about me, he would not be so quick to judge me." "If this person knew what happened to me in college, she would not be so quick to judge me."

I always end by telling the penitent that this is precisely why God's judgments are very different from ours. God has all the data, all the information. God knows exactly why we are like we are. Thus, he is always ready to forgive and to show us his mercy.

God will judge the world with a mercy that is just. That means that all God's judgments are merciful.

People often argue over which is more important,

God's justice or God's mercy. This is a false argument. In his book, *Is This All There Is?*, Gerhard Lohfink writes, "It could be that the question of which carries more weight, God's mercy or God's justice, is becoming a completely false dichotomy. God is completely and all together mercy and just as completely and all together justice—which means that God's justice is mercy and God's mercy is justice."

God's judging wrath does exist, because there is real evil and injustice in the world, and God cannot turn a blind eye to it. But, using Scripture as our guide, we see that, when God threatens to punish or judge harshly, his wrath collapses in favor of showing his people mercy. This is the entire story of God's relationship with Israel. God gets angry, threatens to punish, and then relents. God is furious, ready to wipe out Israel, and then changes his mind.

God always goes from wrath to mercy, from judgment to salvation. It seems that God has no choice but to forgive. God has all the data on us and on everyone and is thus predisposed to forgive and to show mercy, just as we are when we realize that the person in front of us who won't move their car is blind.

We cannot take God's mercy for granted, but we can hope that, when we sin, God will look upon us in the same way that he has treated his people since the beginning—a wrath that always melts into mercy. When we go to meet God, he will not punish us. Rather, his divine mercy could become our judgment, but a judgment that purifies, cleanses, and heals everything in us. This purification, cleansing, and healing is what we have longed for throughout our lives. Why not hope that God's mercy will bring this about in us?

I believe that God will judge me and everyone. But he will judge with mercy — because, when you know all the ins and outs of a person's life as God does, all your judgments are merciful.

*Lord Jesus Christ, Son of the Living God,
have mercy on me, a sinner.*

Being Mercy:
Life in the Key of Gray

As the years go by I become more and more fond of saying, "The older I get the better I look in gray." The phrase is not original. I first heard it from the late Trappist Abbot Bernard Johnson many years ago. One of my very best friends had left the priesthood. He was a great priest, a really popular and effective one. After 19 years of priesthood, celibacy became more and more difficult for him. So, after much prayer and discernment, he left the priesthood and was laicized.

I was about 50 years old at the time and I remember telling Abbot Bernard about the situation. "So, Bernard," I said, "was it a mistake? Was it wrong for him to have become a priest in the first place?" And he said, "Joseph, Joseph, it's not that clear-cut. In fact, the older I get the better I look in gray."

I have never forgotten the abbot's words. Everything that seemed so black or white, good or bad, right or wrong, until I was 50 seems so much grayer now. Of course, some will say I'm wishy-washy, and maybe that's true. But I don't think so. As you get older you begin to see that things are so much more both/and than either/or.

Bishop Frank Caggiano of Bridgeport, says the most important theological word in the Catholic vocabulary may be "and." When the Church talks in "either/or" language we get schisms. The early Church had schisms over the question of whether Christ was human or divine. Those who were able to believe that Jesus is both God and man remained in the Church. Those who believed he was either one or the other left the Church to begin their own. The Church thrives when it talks the language of "both/and": Jesus is true God *and* true man. Mary is Virgin *and* Mother. The Kingdom of God is here *and* yet to come. We are sinners *and* saints. God speaks to us through Scripture *and* tradition. We believe in faith *and* reason.

I used to see so many absolutes in life. Now I think the only absolute I have is the mercy of God.

The Extraordinary Jubilee Year of Mercy taught us that it is the mercy of God more than anything that will save us all.

After a talk I gave recently, someone reported me to a Church authority, saying that I was "too easy on sin." Sin is very real. I sin every day by commission and by omission. That is why I define myself as "a sinner whose sins are forgiven." I don't think that I'm too easy on sin. I know all too well that sin will be my constant companion until I'm in the casket. I will not know a life without sin this side of eternity. I just believe that God's mercy is bigger than any sin.

When I was asked about being too easy on sin, I recalled a story Pope Francis told in February 2016 when he commissioned 800 priests from all over the world, including me, to serve as Missionaries of Mercy. It was about a priest from Argentina who was known to be a great confessor, but who struggled with whether he was forgiving people's sins too easily. He would talk with Jesus about it and then go in front of the tabernacle and say, "Today, I think that I might have forgiven peoples' sins too easily. But let's get this straight. You, dear Jesus, gave me the bad example."

So the only thing I could say in response to my accusation was, "Maybe I am too easy on sin. But Jesus gave me the bad example." Recall the woman caught in adultery. Or the repentant thief on the cross.

Then someone told me of the wonderful line of St. Therese of Lisieux, who went to confession regularly and confessed the smallest of faults. One day her confessor said to her, "But, Sister, you should stop confessing these small, small faults. You don't have to come to confession for such small matters." And she replied, "Who are you to be stingy with a treasure that is not yours?"

Who am I to be stingy with the mercy of God, a treasure that is not mine, a treasure for which I am so grateful? In her novel *Adam Bede*, George Eliot wrote, "When death, the great Reconciler, has come, it is never our tenderness that we repent of, but our severity."

Sometimes I wonder whether I believe so fervently in the relentless mercy of God, his constant forgiveness, his tenderness, his compassion, because it's in my favor to believe in these things, or because they are really true. Then I recall, "This is my Beloved Son, my favor rests on him" (*Matthew 3:17*). As I look at my life, riddled with sin and drenched in grace, it is certainly in my favor, so to speak, to believe in the relentless mercy of God, but that doesn't make it easy. I still have to accept that God's mercy is bigger than my sin. So many of us are tempted to believe the opposite, that our sin might be bigger than God's mercy. Dios mio. That is so not the case.

Then I ask myself, what if I didn't believe in the relentless mercy of God and in his constant forgiveness?

I think I would be stuck in a black-and-white, either/or world with no gray, no both/and. I don't think I would know the freedom of being a child of God that St. Paul writes about in his letters, the freedom Jesus won for us by his death and resurrection. Believing in God's relentless mercy, which breaks through all the black-and-white, either/or categories of life, enables us to live in the key of gray and helps us to accept the freedom that Jesus so desperately wants to give to each one of us.

Lord Jesus Christ, Son of the Living God,
have mercy on me, a sinner.

Being Mercy:
Loving God

I often ask myself if I love God. I know for sure that I want to love God with all my heart and soul and mind and being. But I don't know if I do. I don't know if I can prove that I do.

St. Bernard wrote this about seeking God: "You would not be seeking me if you had not already found me." In a similar fashion, I like to think that I would not want to love God with my whole being if I did not already do so. Please, God, may this be true.

Here is one thing I can point to. In the seventh chapter of the *Gospel of St. Luke*, Jesus goes to dine at Simon's house. While he's there, a sinful woman washes his feet with her tears and dries them with her hair. Jesus says of her, "She has loved much because she has been forgiven much." Well, if this is true of the sinful woman, I hope this can be said of me: "Joe has loved much because he has been forgiven much." And indeed I have been.

Not long ago someone asked me, "Father, if you had your life to live over again, would you?" And my first response was, "No way." The person was surprised and asked why I wouldn't want to live my life over. I said, "There's absolutely no way I could be so blessed a second time around."

Father John Dunne, CSC, used to say, "The worst thing that can happen to you in your life is not that your life plan fails, but that it works, because God's life plan is always so much bigger and better and deeper than anything that you could have ever thought up for yourself." That is certainly the case in my life, which has been filled with more opportunities and blessings than I could ever have imagined. God has been unspeakably good and generous to me and has accompanied me through ups and downs, successes and failures, hopes and disappointments, good times and bad.

I have known more forgiveness than I ever thought I would need. God has shown me a lifetime of mercy, again and again and again. I often wonder how I could have been so lucky, so blessed, so fortunate, so how could I not spend my life in service to God and to others? God has been so reckless with his mercy and forgiveness towards me that I cannot *not* give my life over. God has given me so much that were I not to share it in ministry, I would be hoarding. And all God's gifts are given for the good of the community, not for the individual.

And so I serve as a priest out of deep gratitude for all that God has given me, always hoping that others might experience how rich and blessed and cherished they are by God, how God always has their back, how God has constantly shown them forgiveness and mercy.

I gratefully and willingly celebrate the Eucharist in dorm chapels, at Dillon Hall's Milkshake Mass and the Sunday Mass in Spanish, at the basilica and in parishes, always looking for opportunities to preach about the mercy and love of God.

I hear confessions whenever I'm able because the sacrament of confession remains a unique opportunity to extend God's mercy to others.

I work in Campus Ministry and the Alliance

for Catholic Education, always trying to accompany students on their journey toward God, helping them know that they are immensely cherished and loved and redeemed and forgiven by God.

I live in Dillon Hall with about 300 undergraduates, always trying to be a sign of God's mercy and forgiveness to a generation that thinks it has to "earn" these gifts from God.

I do what I can do because God has given me so much and has been so good and generous to me. In the end, how could I not? When Pope Francis appointed me to be a Missionary of Mercy in February 2016, I said, "God has shown me a lifetime of mercy. How could I not share it with others?"

Do I love God with my whole heart and soul and mind and being? I have been forgiven so much, have been shown so much mercy, that I pray Jesus will say of me what he said of the sinful woman: "Joe has loved much because he has been forgiven much."

Lord Jesus Christ, Son of the Living God,
have mercy on me, a sinner.

Being Mercy:
Return on Investment

A man went to confession every month. One month he said to the priest, "I am not sure of what to say today. I haven't done anything this month." The priest replied, "I am glad you came to confession. Doing nothing is a very serious sin."

Many of us have been brought up to believe that the goal of a Christian life is to avoid making mistakes. While it is important that we try to refrain from doing harmful things, inactivity and not making mistakes is not the goal of our faith.

God created each of us with talents and abilities, and he wants us to use our talents to serve each other and build a community of faith, compassion and mercy. Jesus praises those who try, those who make an attempt, those who risk and those who work.

The Olympic Games feature athletes who spend years perfecting their skills, practicing at odd hours and making many financial and emotional sacrifices to pursue their goals. Olympic athletes have learned to grow from their failures, to see that it is better to have competed and come in second than to protect an imaginary winning record by never competing.

In the Parable of the Talents, *Matthew 25:14-30*, Jesus severely criticizes the servant who congratulated himself for not risking his master's money. Jesus opposes fear. The one who refused to invest the talent he was given didn't fail to invest because he was selfish. He failed to invest because he was afraid. Fear keeps us from being truly alive and from sharing the gifts that God has given us. We cannot listen to those voices of fear. Fear is often the first cousin of sin.

The apostles could have stayed in Palestine after Jesus' resurrection. They could have argued that other people were not quite ready to hear the Gospel. They might have stressed the personal dangers that preaching the Gospel can bring. But no, they went everywhere they could to proclaim the life, death and resurrection of Jesus.

According to tradition, all the apostles except John died as martyrs, most of them outside of Palestine. They rejected a life based on the illusion of avoiding risk. The largest category of saints within our Church is martyrs. Following Jesus may not mean martyrdom for most of us, but it will always involve some risk.

Entrepreneurship teacher Brad Aronson shared this reflection on his blog many years ago, and I have returned to it often:

"Don't be afraid to fail.

You've failed many times, although you may not remember.

You fell down the first time you tried to walk.

You almost drowned the first time you tried to swim.

Did you hit the ball the first time you swung a bat?

Heavy hitters, the ones who hit the most home runs, also strike out a lot.

R.H. Macy failed seven times before his store in New York caught on.

The English author John Creasey got 753 rejection slips before he published 564 books.

Babe Ruth struck out 1,330 times, but he also

hit 714 home runs.
Don't worry about failure.
Worry about the chances that you miss when
you don't even try."

We have all been given gifts from the Lord. The first thing we must do is identify them. Then we must put them at the service of God and of one another.

Investing our gifts in the service of others is a risk—but it is a risk that we must take. Success on a risk is not important. What is important is the freedom that comes from risking.

It's not clear in the parable what talents the owner has given away. But for sure we have all received God's gifts of forgiveness, love, mercy, kindness, grace and faith. These gifts are not given to us to be put in a safe, but to be spread, to be given, and to be offered. Imagine all the mercy and forgiveness God has given you. What good is it if you lock it away in a safe? No! Give it away freely and generously. God will increase it.

He might double or triple your investment, or he might not. That's not important. We are only called to invest what God has given us. He takes care of the rest in his way and in his time.

Doing nothing is, in the end, selfish. Mistakes can always be corrected and forgiven. The Church teaches us that there are certain kinds of success that grow best from the soil of failure. Our faith must give us the courage to act, knowing that God would rather see us make mistakes than do nothing. In *The Joy of the Gospel*, Pope Francis wrote, "I prefer a church which is bruised, hurting and dirty because it has been out on the streets, rather than a church which is unhealthy from being confined and from clinging to its own security. I do not want a church concerned with being at the center and then ends up by being caught up in a web of obsessions and procedures."

We are all called to take a risk on the talents that God has given us. In his mercy, he will be faithful to us.

Lord Jesus Christ, Son of the Living God,
have mercy on me, a sinner.

Being Mercy:
Roman Reflections

**Sunday, April 8, 2018,
the Second Sunday of Easter**
(Divine Mercy Sunday)

Sometime last fall, I received an email from the Vatican informing me that Pope Francis wished to meet with all the Missionaries of Mercy from April 8 to 11 in Rome. From the email, I knew the world had changed forever: In order to register, I had to fill out a Google Form. When you get Google Forms from the Vatican, you know that things have changed!

Our first day began with the Missionaries of Mercy concelebrating Mass with the Holy Father at St. Peter's, up on the esplanade outside the Basilica. That's the first time that I've been that close to the action! As is always the case, Pope Francis gave a great homily. He spoke of the central role of mercy in the life of the Church and in each person's life and harkened back to Thomas, saying that, when Thomas put his fingers into the wounds of Jesus, he received the mercy of God. At the end of the Mass the Holy Father thanked the Missionaries of Mercy for their service to the Church and to the People of God.

After Mass I met up with Father Tony, a priest Cardinal Joe Tobin, CSsR, cardinal archbishop of the Archdiocese of Newark, had introduced me to via email, for a tour of the Vatican.

Tony took me everywhere—to the cupola, to the tombs of the popes, and more. We were walking from the cupola when I saw a simple Ford car parked at the top of a staircase. Tony identified it: "That's the Holy Father's car." We waited for a few moments thinking that the Holy Father would come up a staircase and get in the car, but alas, his driver showed up alone. The pope had decided to walk back to where he lives, so the driver had arrived to move the car. Dang. How amazing would that have been? Just Pope Francis, his driver, Tony and me.

After our almost-encounter, Tony took me to the Domus Santa Marta, where the Holy Father lives. The Domus is the place where the Cardinals stay when they gather to vote for a new pope—something I hope they won't have to do for many more years. Right after Francis was elected pope, he decided to not live in the Apostolic Palace. Rather, he would live at the Domus, alongside many other Vatican employees.

The pope's room is on the second floor, which Tony pointed out from the outside.

"Do you see the only room where the shutters are open and you can see the curtains?"

"Yes," I said. That's the Holy Father's room. They prefer that you keep the shutters closed, Tony explained, but Pope Francis doesn't like that. So he opens the shutters and you can see the curtains.

"No one says anything to him," Tony told me, because he's the Pope!"

At the front door of the Domus, we were greeted by a Swiss guard. Then we went inside the building.

We went into the chapel where the Holy Father celebrates Mass many mornings. I sat in the pope's chair, I kissed the altar that he kisses, and stood at the pulpit where he preaches. I felt like a little kid in a candy store walking all over the chapel and touching everything and thinking about the Holy Father and praying for him. I love him.

Then Tony showed me the dining room where the pope eats. Many other people who live or work at the Domus also eat there, and Tony introduced me to one such diner, Alessandro, while we looked in on the dining room through a window. After Alessandro headed into the dining room, Tony explained who this new acquaintance was: the pope's personal assistant.

"He has more access to the Holy Father than any other person," Tony said.

I had a copy with me of my book, *The Relentless Mercy of God*, for the pope just in case I would see him. This seemed like as good a chance as any, so I asked Tony if I could give the book to Alessandro to give to the pope. He said, "Yes, of course."

So I quickly signed the book to him—"Carissimo Papa Francesco" and some words in Spanish—and bundled it with a small box of South Bend Chocolate Factory sweets that I had bought at the airport. I went into the dining room to give the delivery to Alessandro but couldn't find him. I asked around, and someone said he was in the kitchen. So I went into the kitchen, found him, and asked him to give the book and the chocolates to the Holy Father. He said that he would.

Here I was wandering around this dining room as though I knew what I was doing. The level of security made me chuckle. I was a complete stranger wandering around the dining hall looking for the Holy Father's personal assistant, yet the TSA makes us take off our shoes as though they were filled with South Bend chocolates (or whatever).

Tony eventually followed me into the dining room and showed me the table where the pope has his meals. It seats eight. It's totally simple. It looks like all the other tables in the dining room, though it's off to the side by itself. Alessandro told me that the pope already had lunch. So I went over to the table and took piece of bread from the breadbasket so that I could say that I had a piece of bread from Pope Francis' table. The bread was delicious, of course—perfect crust—but I was in Italy. So, of course, it was going to be perfect crusty bread! I also took a small package of bread sticks (I haven't eaten them yet), and I thought about taking some of the silverware and putting them on eBay. "The pope's fork!" "The pope's spoon!" But I refrained.

After the Domus visit, Tony took me on a diving tour of the beautiful Vatican gardens. (I'd previously only seen them in pictures.) While driving around the gardens, we passed by Pope Emeritus Benedict's home in a monastery where the sisters tasked with taking care of the pope live. I prayed for Pope Emeritus Benedict in gratitude for his tremendous gift of humility to the Church by resigning when he felt that he no longer had the strength and the ability to serve the Church as the Successor of Peter. As we drove past his residence, I thought, "Well, this is the first time that I've ever been by two popes' houses!"

It was quite a day. I won't forget it.

Monday, April 9, 2018,
Monday of the Second Week of Easter

Monday was a very full day. Our morning classes were at the Pontifical Lateran University, an impressively modern 245-year-old institution near the Cathedral Basilica of St. John Lateran. After lunch we broke into language groups for more lectures and Masses at different local parishes. I went with the English-speaking group, but I should have gone to the talk in Spanish. I can understand Spanish better than I can understand British!

The best part of the day was listening to five of my confreres—from Italy, South Korea, Panama, Oceania, and Guinea—talk about their experience serving as Missionaries of Mercy. I was really inspired by their reflections and comments. The Missionary of Mercy from Oceania spent the entire Jubilee Year of Mercy traveling in a camper to dozens of communities that do not have a resident priest and who might see a priest just five or six times a year. In each place he would show up on Saturday, celebrate Mass on Sunday, and then sit in the parish church for 10-12 hours every day for the week to meet with anyone who wished to come in. As the week went on in each place, more and more people came to the church to talk with him.

In Panama, the Missionary of Mercy set up a confession station at the country's busiest railroad station. He spoke about how many people came to confession when they saw a priest sitting there with his stole on.

I was truly inspired by the generosity and holiness of these priests. And I came away with a few ideas how we might make this sacrament of mercy more available to our students at Notre Dame, especially to those who have not gone to confession for years and, for whatever reason, don't go to the Basilica.

Tuesday, April 10, 2018, Tuesday of the Second Week of Easter

On Tuesday our class was in the Sala Regia of the Apostolic Palace. The first talk was from Archbishop Rino Fisichella, the president of the Pontifical Council for the Promotion of the New Evangelization. I like him. He gave a good talk.

This was followed by a talk from Pope Francis, who was, as always, outstanding. After he walked into the room (smiling as he always does), Archbishop Fisichella welcomed him and told him that we are the Missionaries of Mercy whom Pope Francis had appointed during the Year of Mercy. Of course, the pope knew this, but it's part of the protocol of how these things are.

"Holy Father, not all the Missionaries are here who were here two years ago," the archbishop said.

"Some have gone home to paradise, some have been named bishops, and some could not make the trip."

Without missing a beat, Pope Francis said, "I hope that the ones who have become bishops are still merciful." He smiled and we all laughed.

Then the Holy Father gave his talk. It is so clear that mercy is not a program or a project for him. IT IS EVERYTHING. Mercy is not something abstract. It is a way of life, a way of living that brings everything together. Francis often says that he wishes "mercy" were a verb because it functions like one. He told us why, even though the Jubilee Year of Mercy ended in November of 2016, he asked us to continue as Missionaries of Mercy. He said that during the Year of Mercy, he received so many testimonies about people whose lives were changed by interacting with a Missionary of Mercy that he decided to ask us to continue on indefinitely. He reminded us to be gentle, to smile, to be welcoming to penitents, to not ask unnecessary questions, which most of them are. He explained that, when a penitent comes to confession, he or she has already had an encounter of love with the Lord who has brought them to this place. The Church can never put any kind of obstacle to anyone who wishes to come to this sacrament, pointing out that, when the Prodigal Son decided to return to his father, he did not have to go through customs or immigration. Francis reminded us that it is Christ who waits in the confessional, Christ who welcomes, Christ who forgives, Christ who blesses. I truly could have listened to him for hours. He also asked us to do as much as we can to hear confessions. He believes that this sacrament is an inexhaustible sign of God's mercy in the Church and in the world.

At the end of the talk, he said, "I want to meet each one of you and shake your hand and thank you for your service to the Church. Most people want to meet the pope, but I want to meet you." I was one of the first to greet him since I had pushed my way up from the fifth row to the third. I shook his hand, told him that I loved him, and hugged him and kissed his cheek. I just happened to be wearing my Pope Francis socks that day, so I pulled up my pant leg and showed the socks to him. He smiled.

I can't even imagine how exhausting it would be to shake hands with almost 600 people as he did. He said that he wanted to do this to show his regard for our work. He made me cry. Imagine—the Holy Father thanking us for our work. But this is vintage Francis. This is who he is. I love him.

Then we all celebrated Mass with him inside St. Peter's Basilica at the Chair of Peter. We all processed into the Basilica from the entrance, which is no small feat—I think that I did my 10,000 steps for the day just processing in and out.

Pope Francis is man of prayer. He truly prays during the Mass. You can just see it. After communion, he sat in his chair and was absorbed in prayer. As luck would have it, I was seated directly in front of where he sat and where he preached from, just two rows back. I was moved by his homily as he talked about the effectiveness of gentle and kind priests.

After Mass we were each given a beautiful gift from the Holy Father. It is a bronze plaque depicting the return of the Prodigal Son—a replica of one of the "squares" in the holy door.

Tuesday was another incredible day that I will never forget.

Wednesday, April 11, 2018,
Wednesday of the Second Week of Easter

On Wednesday our class was once again at the Pontifical Lateran University. Archbishop Octavio Ruiz, the number two guy in the Pontifical Council for the Promotion of the New Evangelization, gave a great talk. (I first met Archbishop Ruiz here at Notre Dame two years ago when he was on campus to give a talk.) Following this, we all concelebrated Mass at the Cathedral Basilica of St. John Lateran. It is the oldest and highest-ranking of the four papal major basilicas, giving it the unique title of "archbasilica". Because it is the oldest public church in the city of Rome, and houses the *cathedra* of the Bishop of Rome, the pope, it has the title of ecumenical mother church of the Catholic faithful. Archbishop Rino Fisichella presided and preached.

It's clear that the Holy Father will continue preaching about mercy, offering mercy, and making mercy the hallmark, so to speak, of his entire Pontificate. He constantly says that God gave him mercy, that God has always been merciful to him. I know that same reality. God showed me his mercy.

I left our gathering evermore grateful to God for my vocation to the priesthood and more convinced than ever of my unworthiness for so great a gift. Like St. Paul, I say of myself, I am the worst of all sinners. And God has shown me his mercy. I am beyond grateful to serve the Church as a Missionary of Mercy for as long as Pope Francis asks us to do so.

Lord Jesus Christ, Son of the Living God,
have mercy on me, a sinner.

Being Mercy:
The Church's Ritual

O ne of my most memorable proofs of the power of liturgy comes from early in my priesthood It was 1990, and, at 35, I had just been named pastor of St. John Vianney, a Holy Cross parish in Goodyear, Arizona. I was surprised, shocked even, to have received the appointment, not knowing then that the provincial had already been told "no"—something I was not yet smart enough to say!—by three priests before asking me. A few weeks into my tenure (in what I can only hope is a coincidence), the United States went to war.

The Persian Gulf War broke out in August of 1990, with one of our parishioners, a young man named Eliseo Felix, among the troops. Eliseo had joined the Marines in May after his high school graduation and I arrived in July, so the two of us had never met. But, a few months into the conflict, the news arrived that he had been killed in the war.

The death of anyone in any place is tragic, but in a small town where everyone knows everyone, it seems even more so. Goodyear was a town of less than 8,000 people. It seemed that the entire town learned of his death in a matter of moments, leaving everyone in sorrow and grief.

I don't remember who told me that Eliseo Felix had been killed, but I know I was told on Sunday morning before the first Mass of the day. And I remember being told that no one knew when his body would be brought back to the States.

I knew that the first thing that I wanted to do was visit his mother, Hortencia. And the other thing that I had to do was to gather the parish for Mass to pray for the repose of his soul and for his family and for peace. Once the Sunday Masses were over, I went straight to Hortencia's house and asked her: Since we did not know when her son's body would be returned, could we have a Mass for him on Monday night? She said that she would be grateful. So we planned to have a Mass for him on Monday night. The word got out right away.

Hortencia was a quiet, shy woman, and now she was in grief. The news around this event was relentless, and every news station in Phoenix wanted to get to her and talk with her—even calling me to ask how to get in touch with Hortencia. Soon, of course, they learned of the Mass at St. John Vianney. The news stations and cameras were there hours before the Mass was scheduled to start at 7 p.m.

The Mass was beautiful and the Church was filled with hundreds of people, extending even into the atrium. After Mass I drove Hortencia back to her home, and we had a conversation.

"Father, when I heard that *m'hijito* [my son] had been killed, nothing made sense to me," she said. "I didn't know which end was up. I didn't know which end was down. I didn't know how to think. I couldn't pray. I didn't know what to say. I could barely function. And that's how it was until Monday night when I walked into the church. And when you said, 'The Lord be with you,' I knew what to say. When you said, 'Lord, have mercy,' I knew to respond, 'Lord, have mercy.' When you said, 'A reading from the holy Gospel according to John,' I knew what to respond.

When I went to communion and you said 'the Body of Christ,' I knew to say 'Amen.' When it was time to stand, I knew to stand. When it was time to kneel, I knew to kneel."

This is the power of liturgy, of good liturgy. When we don't know what to say, the Church puts words in our mouths. When we are completely incapable of thinking, of knowing what to do, the liturgy of the Church gives us words and gestures and movements. Without knowing it, Hortencia explained to me in 10 minutes the real power of the Church's liturgy. It can help us move and function when we otherwise, for whatever reasons, are unable to do so.

The mercy of God is always and forever operating in us, when we are aware of it and when we are not aware of it, when we know we need it and when we don't think about how much we need it.

Pope Francis says that we need to be reminded as often as possible that the name of God is mercy, and, in the liturgy, there are many reminders. Each time we celebrate the Eucharist, we hear of the Lord's mercy for us again and again.

"Lord, have mercy. Christ, have mercy. Lord, have mercy."

"Lamb of God, you take away the sins of the world, have mercy on us."

"Remember also our brothers and sisters who have fallen asleep in the hope of the resurrection, all who have died in your mercy."

"By the help of your mercy, we may be always free from sin and safe from all distress."

May we never tire of hearing these words spoken to each one of us. May we always be open to the inexhaustible mercy of God and then share that mercy with those near and far.

Lord Jesus Christ, Son of the Living God,
have mercy on me, a sinner.

Being Mercy:
The Crisis

———

O ver the summer, two bishops from Pennsylvania told me about an investigation unfolding in
their state's courts. The state attorney general had
been conducting an investigation into sexual abuse
committed by priests against minors, and the grand
jury was expected to release a report sometime soon.

It's going to be very ugly, the bishops told me.
Really ugly.

Having lived through the 2002 sexual abuse crisis
first uncovered by the *Boston Globe*, I did not think
this case would be much different from that one. I
was wrong.

As the release date of the grand jury's report drew
closer, I read a statement from another bishop in

Pennsylvania who had told the people of his diocese, "Get ready. This is going to be awful."

No amount of getting ready could have prepared anyone for what the grand jury report revealed on Tuesday, August 14. I am from Pennsylvania. I did not want to read the report. But at the same time I could not stop reading it once I started. Seeing the names of priests that had served in my home parish was painful, horrible.

Since that horrible day, I have spent hours and hours reading the Pennsylvania report and dozens of articles, commentaries, op-eds and viewpoint pieces about the abuse. Every article has a link to another article, then another. I find myself unable to stop clicking on the links.

As a priest, I am embarrassed and ashamed by what other priests have done. I am angry, outraged, infuriated at what some priests have done to children, the most vulnerable among us. On the first day of Welcome Weekend here on campus, I could not bring myself to wear my Roman collar. I was too ashamed to be seen as a priest, a vocation that I love with all my heart and soul. Over these past weeks I have returned constantly to the words of St. Paul in his *Second Letter*

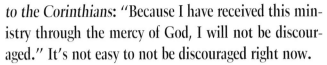

to the Corinthians: "Because I have received this ministry through the mercy of God, I will not be discouraged." It's not easy to not be discouraged right now.

In my clicking through the countless links responding to the crisis, I have seen many articles and video clips that feature bishops and priests talking about all that the grand jury report revealed. In them, the author or speaker expresses his outrage and voices sorrow for the victims and their families, but often, these bishops and priests move into a defensive position. The moment that happens, I stop reading or listening. This is not the time to be defensive.

I hear defensive comments like this: *Yes, but almost all of the abuse detailed in the report happened 50–70 years ago.*

You know what that means? That means the wounds are 50-70 years old. It is true that, since 2002, safeguards have been put into place—in dioceses, in Catholic parishes, in Catholic schools—that have cut down extensively on child sexual abuse. We are grateful for this. But the fact that abuse may be less common now does not negate the decades of pain that the victims of 50 or 70 years ago have had to live with.

Pope Francis said in his August 20 letter to the People of God, "We have realized that these wounds never disappear and that they require us forcefully to condemn these atrocities and join forces in uprooting this culture of death; these wounds never go away." The pope has drawn criticism of his own in the past few weeks, but I agree with this message from his letter. We must admit our guilt and not be defensive.

Another defensive comment I have heard goes something like this: *Well, the Catholic Church does not have a corner or a market on child sexual abuse.*

This is true. The insidious crime of child abuse has unfolded in public school settings, in neighborhoods, and perpetrators have come from all professions and walks of life, the priesthood perhaps no more or less than any other. But priests have promised to give their lives to God, to the Gospel, to the People of God. While there are many other abusers, those other abusers have not promised to give their lives to God, to preach the Gospel, and to serve the faithful. This does not make priests better. Rather, it makes us more accountable. We should be shaking in our shoes because of the trust that people put in us. We must admit our guilt and our wrongdoing, not be defensive about it.

With everything inside of me, I love the Church. And I love being a priest. I will be grateful to God forever for the gift of a vocation to the priesthood—in fact, I will never be able to be grateful enough. I lament that the trust in and love for the Church that I had as a child will not be restored to the Church in my lifetime. This makes me so sad.

This is no time to play defense. Rather, it is a time for bishops and priests to confess that we have greatly sinned, in what we have done and in what we have failed to do, through our fault, through our fault, through our most grievous fault. It is time to beg God's forgiveness and the forgiveness of those who have been abused. It is time for bishops and priests to weep, to cry, and to truly accompany the abused and their families, if they will let us.

It is time for us to cry out:
Lord, have mercy. Christ, have mercy.
Lord, have mercy.

Lord Jesus Christ, Son of the Living God,
have mercy on me, a sinner.

Being Mercy:
The Eucharist at the Border

Some years ago, on November 2, the Feast of All Souls, I had the great privilege of concelebrating Mass at the US/Mexico border between Ciudad Juarez in Mexico and Anapra, New Mexico in the United States. It was one of the most moving and powerful Masses of my life. Each year Mass is celebrated on the border in honor of all those who have died trying to cross it. I began crying before the Mass started and cried off and on during the entire Mass.

As we got close to where the Mass was to be celebrated, we began to see Border Patrol trucks and officers everywhere.

The Mass is celebrated with half the altar on the United States side of the border and the other half of the altar on the Mexico side of the border. An 18-foot-high fence along the Rio Grande marks the border in this part of Texas, so the two "halves" of the altar are separated by this physical barrier as well as the jurisdictional one. All along the fence, white crosses displayed the names of people who have died trying to cross the border.

In addition to the Border Patrol officers stationed every 20 feet or so, the Mass was attended by hundreds of people both in Mexico and the United States. On the Mexico side, the Mass was led by the Bishop Renato Ascension León, Bishop of Ciudad Juarez, and about 20 priests. On the US side, Bishop Ricardo Ramirez (emeritus of Las Cruces, New Mexico) and Bishop Armando Ochoa (of Fresno, and former Bishop of El Paso) officiated alongside about 15 priests.

I could not stop staring at the fence with the altar on both sides. Here we were, gathered as one Body of Christ, yet divided into two by a fence. While the Eucharist speaks of our oneness in Christ, of the One Bread and the One Cup, of inclusion, the fence speaks of the opposite—division and separation and exclusion.

The entrance procession began with people on

both sides of the fence carrying the typical symbols of an entrance procession — first the Crucifix and then the image of Our Lady of Guadalupe. Following were the flags of both countries and then items that people carry when they try to cross—water, food, shoes and a backpack. I don't know why but when I saw the backpack and the shoes I could not stop crying.

The Mass was bilingual with beautiful music. The first reading was read in Spanish by someone from the Mexico side of the border, then the second reading was read in English by someone from the US side. I was struck over and over by the absurdity of borders, of one Body of Christ divided into two.

Bishop Ramirez preached a great bilingual homily, and the Eucharistic Prayer was particularly powerful. The bishops from both sides shared the prayer, creating another powerful sight—Bishops, the Successors of the Apostles on both sides of the border, united in the Eucharist, divided by a fence.

At the Kiss of Peace, I wept as people on both sides of the fence put their fingers through the holes in the fence to touch the fingers of their sisters and brothers on the other side. I cannot described what I experienced at the moment that I joined them. It was perhaps the deepest longing I have ever known for justice, for peace, for unity, for acceptance, for inclusion.

I wanted to offer the Peace of Christ to some of the Border Patrol officers. But I was hesitant, not knowing how it would be received. Now I wish so much that I had done it.

Of course, the communion rite was also powerful—the One Bread and the One Cup shared by fellow Catholics on both sides of a fence, a division that must break God's heart.

After communion there was silence to honor and pray for all who have died trying to cross the border—about 5,000 people in the past 15 years.

The Mass ended with the usual blessing and we all sang the great Easter hymn "Resucitó" by Kiko Arguello. After the Mass, I spotted another powerful sight, as two groups of Dominican nuns, both dressed in the same habit, approached each other from the two sides of the border and spoke through the fence.

My mind was flooded throughout the mass with the faces of undocumented people that I have worked with during the 19 years that I served as a pastor—faces from St. John Vianney in Arizona and faces from Holy Redeemer in Oregon. I prayed for these people. I prayed for real and honest immigration reform in our day. I still pray for this now.

Again, I want to say that this was one of the most powerful Masses that I have ever attended in all my life. Seeing one altar divided by a fence with the People of God on both sides—people for whom Jesus gave his life—will be forever engraved on my mind and in my heart.

Concelebrating this Mass reminded me so powerfully that immigration is about people. People. Families. Children. Siblings. Parents. People. If we all recognized our common need for the mercy of God and saw that mercy is at the heart of the world, I believe that we would all work toward immigration reform. Borders would be less important and inclusion would become more a way of life, a way of acting, a way of being.

.

Lord Jesus Christ, Son of the Living God,
have mercy on me, a sinner.

Being Mercy:
The Sister, the Principals and the Prisoners

When the Extraordinary Year of Mercy proclaimed by Pope Francis ended on November 20, 2016, he closed the Holy Door in Rome. On that same day, the Holy Father issued a letter called "Misericordia et Misera." In that letter he asked the Missionaries of Mercy, whom he had commissioned and sent forth the previous Ash Wednesday, to continue serving the Church in that special role even after the year had ended.

I was in Rome that day. It's a day that I will never forget, because I got to talk with Pope Francis, to hug him and to tell him how much I loved him.

Though I have fewer commitments now than I did during the Year of Mercy, I continue to serve the Church as a Missionary of Mercy in any way that is asked of me.

Recently I gave more or less the same talk, focused on the Parables of Mercy, to three very different groups. In each case—in a convent, before an archdiocese and in an Indiana state prison—I thought of the varied life experiences that people bring as they listen to the Gospel. As the saying goes: "Where you stand depends on where you sit."

First, I had the wonderful privilege of preaching a Lenten Day of Recollection on the parables to about 80 Sisters of the Holy Cross at Saint Mary's College. The group included aged and infirmed sisters, many of whom watched from their rooms in the infirmary via closed-circuit TV; some active sisters; a number of novices from many of the countries where the Sisters work and serve; and several Holy Cross Associates.

What a blessing to be able to speak to these women who have dedicated—or are about to dedicate—their lives to serving God and the Church. Many were nodding and taking notes as I talked. I cannot say this for sure, but I would imagine that, as I discussed the Parable of the Prodigal Son, most would have identified with the older brother. I say this gently. The sisters know their need for mercy, but like so many good and well-behaved people, they might only know it intellectually.

The Parable of the Workers and the Vineyard reveals a landowner who goes out at 6 a.m., at 9 a.m., at noon, at 3 p.m. and an hour before quitting time, always in search of more workers for his vineyard. At the end of the day, he pays each the same amount. In this moment where the last becomes first, the parable—a bit like the Prodigal Son—reveals the Father's urgent concern for the outcasts, the marginalized, the idle. Grace and help are just as available for the well-behaved as for these characters at the margins—it's just that the well-behaved often do not know it.

To the laborer who began work at 6 a.m., it seemed unfair to be paid the same amount as those who arrived just before closing time. Again, I can't say this for sure, but I have a feeling, had the Sisters been working in that vineyard, most would have been in the group who arrived at the crack of dawn.

Three days after the Saint Mary's event, I preached at a similar Day of Recollection for 110 principals and school leaders from the Archdiocese of Milwaukee, a wonderful group of people who have given their lives to educate young children and teenagers, who have devoted countless hours to Catholic education. By and large, principals are practical people. They deal with all sorts of different students and families. As they listened to the Parable of the Prodigal Son, many might have been thinking of the children in their schools—which child is which brother?

In the Parable of the Workers and the Vineyard, these administrators would probably have sided with those who complained about receiving the same pay for 12 hours as the group that worked for one hour. This kind of parable would make the folks in the Office of Human Resources go crazy!

A few days later, I had the unique privilege of talking about the Parables of Mercy to six prisoners at the Westville Prison, about an hour west of South Bend. What an incredible experience to sit around a table with six guys and talk about these parables. One of the first things that I noticed is that they all wear nametags, each reading "OFFENDER" on one line and the person's last name on the next. I did not like that. Imagine being known, and worse, thinking of yourself as OFFENDER. God never thinks of us in those terms. God can only think of us as his beloved children.

As I read Luke's Parable of the Prodigal Son, it was clear that the men around the table all identified with the younger brother. Some felt the connection less than others—in the prison hierarchy of crimes, someone imprisoned for drug trafficking may feel less "prodigal" than someone else imprisoned for murder —but each of the men had insightful responses. One guy said, "I always have thought of myself a bit like the older brother in this sense. I grew up in a very diverse world. And so I grew up without racism. I prided myself in not being a racist. And then it hit me: I can't stand racists. And that's just as bad a being one."

Since many of the men in prison might have been those hired last, they were delighted to learn of a landowner who goes out looking for more workers even at the 11th hour. They were happy to know of a leader who cares so deeply about everyone that he does whatever he can so that no one is lost.

I loved listening to the questions and thoughts and sharing of these men in prison. It's clear that they know their need for mercy, and not just intellectually. They know their need for mercy in the flesh. It's real for them. They want it so badly that they can taste it. For the men in prison, mercy is not abstract, but concrete and real. And they want it.

Each group—the Sisters, the Principals, and the Prisoners—were a little surprised that both the older and the younger brother have the same need for mercy. The younger brother thinks that he's too dirty to receive mercy while the older brother thinks that he's too good to need mercy. All three groups were surprised to know that whether we think that we are too good to need mercy or to bad to receive mercy, the fallacy is the same. Both sons disrespected the father by not believing in all that he wanted to give them.

As I pointed out to each group, and I'm very fond of saying, it doesn't matter who you are. In the end, it is the mercy of God that will save us all. Because God is faithful, he will offer his mercy to us in as many ways as possible until we accept it. Sit where you will, stand where you will—God will have his way with us.

One day we will accept his mercy, even long for his mercy…and let it save us.

Lord Jesus Christ, Son of the Living God,
have mercy on me, a sinner.

Being Mercy:
Concluding Thoughts

When Pope Francis closed the Holy Door on November 20, 2016, signifying the end of the Extraordinary Jubilee Year of Mercy, he said "Mercy cannot become a mere parenthesis in the life of the Church; it constitutes her very existence, through which the profound truths of the Gospel are made manifest and tangible. Everything is revealed in mercy; everything is resolved in the merciful love of the Father." And so it is. The mercy of God is the foundation of the Church. I especially love the phrase "everything is resolved in the merciful love of the Father." There are many things that cannot be understood, reconciled, explained in this life. So it helps me to think that they can all be held together in the merciful love of the Father.

The Year of Mercy ended more than two years ago, and yet its message still continues to have a profound impact on the life of the Church and beyond. Each day I am more and more grateful that Pope Francis chose me to serve as a Missionary of Mercy. The mercy of God has transformed and is transforming my life. I want to know the mercy of God more and more and I want to spread that mercy wherever and however I can.

We are living in a world, and even in a Church, which is profoundly divided. Everything seems to boil down to A vs. B. A is opposed to B. B is better than A. A is smarter than B. B is holier than A. A is correct and B is incorrect. And on and on and on. No matter the differences and divisions, the truth is A and B both need mercy. If A and B could both recognize this and rejoice in this, everyone would win and divisions and barriers and walls would break down more and more.

Recognizing our common need for mercy can save us. No matter who we are, no matter what we do, no matter what we have done or not done, no matter if we are the older brother or the younger brother or both brothers in the Parable of the Merciful Father, we would know our common need for mercy. Knowing our common need for mercy would reduce or possibly even eliminate our divisions. For sure we would be able to be more open and understanding and accepting of one another.

When it comes to mercy, we have all been given a great share in the banquet. We have been given so much by God.

The famous Trappist Monk Thomas Merton, OCSO, says it so well when he writes, "Mercy within mercy within mercy…" At the center is God's mercy enfolding us in God's embrace and inviting us to embrace one another in mercy and in love.

The only claim that I have for this is that I am a sinner whose sins are forgiven. It is from and in this self-understanding that I have tried to serve the Church as a Missionary of Mercy. And it is from this that I have written and shared these reflections.

I never imagined in 100 years that I would write a book…and a second book would never have seemed a possibility. I have received so much mercy from God that it seems ungrateful to not write about mercy.

I hope that in reading these simple reflections and in thinking about them and in praying over them that you might allow this mercy to enter your life more fully and more deeply. Though we might tire of asking God for forgiveness, God never tires of offering us forgiveness. Pope Francis writes, "God is merciful (cf. Ex 34:6); his mercy lasts forever (cf. Ps 136). From generation to generation, it embraces all those who trust in him and it changes them, by bestowing a share in his very life."

Lord Jesus Christ, Son of the Living God,
have mercy on me, a sinner.